Diet recommendations for liver c

Please check these recommendations alwa
consultant, therapist, doctor or dietician. Th
ingredients are supporting the conventional medical therapy.
The calorie disclosures of fresh ingredients (fruit and vegetables) vary according to quality and time of harvest. The contents were checked by a dietician and a nutrition consultant for the Traditional Chinese Medicine (TCM).

Author:
©2019 Josef Miligui
www.ebns.at

Source:
The lists are created from the EBNS database for nutritional counseling. The database is used by dietitians, therapists and doctors for advising the patient / client.

Literature:
The specialist literature and the training documents of the German and Austrian dietary and traditional Chinese medicine serve as a knowledge base. We have used the documents as a basis of knowledge, adapted it to our experience and completed them.
http://di-book.com

Production and publishing:
BoD – Books on Demand, Norderstedt
ISBN: 9783746043135

(Book: E028)

Diet recommendations for DIETETICS - Gastrointestinal tract - Liver, gallbladder, bile ducts - Liver cirrhosis

1 Treatment strategy 3
2 Avoid 4
3 Breakfast 4
4 Snack 5
5 Lunch 5
6 Afternoon 6
7 Dinner 6
8 Any time 7
9 Recipes 8
   9.1 Apple sauce with raisins 8
   9.2 Asparagus Cream Soup 8
   9.3 Banana Soymilk 9
   9.4 Barley mash with berries 10
   9.5 Basic recipe for a beef broth (clear) 11
   9.6 Basic recipe for a chicken broth worming 12
   9.7 Basic recipe for a reissue soup (Congee) 12
   9.8 Basic recipe for a vegetable soup, nutritious 13
   9.9 Black root with yogurt 14
   9.10 Blueberry puree 15
   9.11 Carrot and rice gruel soup 15
   9.12 Carrots with potato foam 16
   9.13 Celery soup 16
   9.14 Chicken soup with egg yolk and parsley 17
   9.15 Compote from apples 18
   9.16 Compote from rhubarb 18
   9.17 Corn coffee with cardamom 18
   9.18 Cottage cheese with steamed fruit 19
   9.19 Cranberry juice 19
   9.20 Cranberry yogurt mix 20
   9.21 Fennel and potato gratin 20
   9.22 Frozen pineapple juice 21
   9.23 Grated apple 21
   9.24 Kohlrabi in chervil sauce with potatoes 22
   9.25 Kohlrabi Potatoes mash 23
   9.26 Mango banana yoghurt drink ice cold 23
   9.27 Nettle-chard soup 24
   9.28 Noodle soup - Also for babies from 10 month 24
   9.29 Oat Congee 26

9.30	Potato with dandelion salad	26
9.31	Pumpkin soup	27
9.32	Pumpkin-yoghurt soup	27
9.33	Puréed banana	28
9.34	Rhubarb and apple jelly	28
9.35	Rice congee with carrots and fennel	29
9.36	Rice with parsnips	30
9.37	Ricepudding	30
9.38	Roasted millet with Celery sticks	31
9.39	Rosemary Potatoes	31
9.40	Semolina porridge with banana	32
9.41	Soup with egg yolk	33
9.42	Tea from peppermint with white sugar	33
9.43	Tea Green tea	34
9.44	Tea mixture against general exhaustion	34
9.45	Tea rooibos	35
9.46	Tomato with mozzarella	35
10	Effects of food	36
10.1	Use ingredients: recommendable	36
10.2	Use ingredients: yes	36
10.3	Use ingredients: little	39
10.4	Do not use contra-acting foods	41
11	Complementary	44
11.1	xx	44
12	Basics of Nutrition	45
12.1	Nutrition	45
12.2	Recipes	47
12.3	Foodstuffs	47
12.4	Herbs	48
13	Other dietic-books	49
14	EBNS - Software for nutritional counseling	51

1 Treatment strategy

Ensure optimal supply of nutrients and energy.
Individual intolerances take into account, strict alcohol ban!
Adjust the deviations in the liquid- and electrolyte-balance.
Prevent body's own protein degradation, avoid encephalopathy.
Protein-rich diet (vegetable protein is better than animal protein).

2 Avoid
Alcohol, meat.

3 Breakfast

kkal. per serving

Apple sauce with raisins	73
Banana Soymilk	125
Barley mash with berries	112
Blueberry puree	10
Carrot and rice gruel soup	101
Carrots with potato foam	316
Celery soup	101
Compote from apples	67
Compote from rhubarb	48
Corn coffee with cardamom	3
Cottage cheese with steamed fruit	214
Cranberry juice	43
Cranberry yogurt mix	57
Frozen pineapple juice	29
Grated apple	120
Grated carrots with apple	74
Kohlrabi in chervil sauce with potatoes	187
Kohlrabi Potatoes mash	278
Mango banana yoghurt drink ice cold	121
Noodle soup	236
Oat Congee	162
Potato cream with herbs and fresh cheese	217
Pumpkin-yoghurt soup	68
Puréed banana	144
Rhubarb and apple jelly	180
Rice congee with carrots and fennel	131
Rice with parsnips	206
Ricepudding	316
Roasted millet with Celery sticks	400
Rosemary Potatoes	188
Semolina porridge with banana	307
Soup with egg yolk	173
Tea from peppermint with white sugar	7
Tea Green tea	2

4 Snack

Apple sauce with raisins ... 73
Barley mash with berries ... 112
Carrots with potato foam ... 316
Grated carrots with apple ... 74
Kohlrabi Potatoes mash ... 278
Ricepudding ... 316

5 Lunch

Asparagus Cream Soup ... 240
Banana Soymilk ... 125
Black root with yogurt ... 319
Blueberry puree ... 10
Carrot and rice gruel soup ... 101
Celery soup ... 101
Chicken soup with egg yolk and parsley ... 117
Compote from apples ... 67
Compote from rhubarb ... 48
Corn coffee with cardamom ... 3
Cottage cheese with steamed fruit ... 214
Cranberry juice ... 43
Cranberry yogurt mix ... 57
Fennel and potato gratin ... 147
Frozen pineapple juice ... 29
Grated apple ... 120
Kohlrabi in chervil sauce with potatoes ... 187
Mango banana yoghurt drink ice cold ... 121
Nettle-chard soup ... 52
Noodle soup ... 236
Oat Congee ... 162
Potato cream with herbs and fresh cheese ... 217
Pumpkin soup ... 104
Pumpkin-yoghurt soup ... 68
Puréed banana ... 144
Rhubarb and apple jelly ... 180
Rice with parsnips ... 206
Ricepudding ... 316
Roasted millet with Celery sticks ... 400
Rosemary Potatoes ... 188
Semolina porridge with banana ... 307
Soup with egg yolk ... 173
Tea from peppermint with white sugar ... 7

Tea Green tea 2
Tomato with mozzarella 436

6 Afternoon

Apple sauce with raisins 73
Barley mash with berries 112
Carrots with potato foam 316
Grated carrots with apple 74
Kohlrabi Potatoes mash 278
Ricepudding 316

7 Dinner

Asparagus Cream Soup 240
Black root with yogurt 319
Blueberry puree 10
Carrots with potato foam - Also for babies from 8 months 316
Celery soup 101
Compote from apples 67
Compote from rhubarb 48
Corn coffee with cardamom 3
Cranberry juice 43
Cranberry yogurt mix 57
Fennel and potato gratin 147
Frozen pineapple juice 29
Grated apple 120
Kohlrabi in chervil sauce with potatoes 187
Kohlrabi Potatoes mash 278
Mango banana yoghurt drink ice cold 121
Noodle soup - Also for babies from 10 month 236
Oat Congee 162
Pumpkin soup 104
Pumpkin-yoghurt soup 68
Rice with parsnips 206
Ricepudding 316
Roasted millet with Celery sticks 400
Rosemary Potatoes 188
Semolina porridge with banana 307
Tea from peppermint with white sugar 7
Tea Green tea 2
Tomato with mozzarella 436

8 Any time

Apple sauce with raisins 73
Basic recipe for a reissue soup (Congee) 140
Blueberry puree 10
Carrot and rice gruel soup 101
Carrots with potato foam... 316
Compote from apples 67
Compote from rhubarb.. 48
Corn coffee with cardamom... 3
Cranberry juice 43
Cranberry yogurt mix 57
Frozen pineapple juice.. 29
Grated apple 120
Kohlrabi Potatoes mash.. 278
Mango banana yoghurt drink ice cold 121
Oat Congee 162
Puréed banana 144
Rice congee with carrots and fennel 131
Rice with parsnips.. 206
Ricepudding 316
Roasted millet with Celery sticks 400
Semolina porridge with banana 307
Tea from peppermint with white sugar 7
Tea Green tea.. 2
Tea rooibos 0

9 Recipes

(rec.) = You can use more.
(little) = You should use less than specified
(no) omit.

9.1 Apple sauce with raisins

Stops diarrhea, promotes digestion, appetizing, relieves diarrhea, activates carbohydrate metabolism.
Cooking time approx. 25 min
Allergens: O
10 portions to 115g. / 74kcal. - (carb:96% / prot:4%)
100g.=64kcal. / protein 0,32g. fat:0,43g.
µg. - Ph:0,14 Na:0,04 Ka:1,59 Mg:0,06 Ca:0,08 Fe:0 Zn:0 Col.:0 Hsr.:0,14

Quantity of ingredients:
Apple (sweet) 2,2 lbs / 1000g. (little)
Water 1/2 cup / 100g. (yes)
Raisins 1/8 lbs - 2oz / 50g. (little)

Cooking instructions:
Wash, peel and quarter the apples and remove the core. Put the apples with the water in a pot. Wash the raisins with hot water and add them. Cook at low heat for about 10 minutes, then allow to cool. For children up to 10 months, mash in the blender finely. For the larger ones, crush with the potato steamer. Fill and seal in a freezer or empty yoghurt jug. Close the yoghurt jug. Freeze in the shock freezer.
If necessary, thaw at room temperature for about 6 hours. (Lasting about 4 months).
The fruit mousse is intended as dessert or intermediate meal. It has an anti-digestive effect. In case of diarrhea give better banana.

9.2 Asparagus Cream Soup

Diuretic, improves blood circulation, prevents cancer, laxative, antiparasitic, stimulates liver function, good to fight loss of appetite, flatulence, rheumatism, heartburn.
Cooking time approx. 45 min
Allergens: ACG
2 portions to 409,5g. / 240kcal. - (carb:21% / prot:79%)
100g.=58,61kcal. / protein 5,2g. fat:19,85g.
µg. - Ph:9,44 Na:1,5 Ka:15,8 Mg:1,6 Ca:6,23 Fe:0,13 Zn:0,08 Col.:9,84 Hsr.:2,42

Quantity of ingredients:
Asparagus (green or white) 5/8 oz / 200g. (rec.)
Water 2 cup / 500g. (yes)
Rapeseed oil 3 table spoons / 30g. (little)
Wheat flour 2 table spoons / 10g. (yes)
Chicken yolk 1 piece / 25g. (little)
Cow's milk (whole milk 3.5% fat) 1 table spoon / 15g. (little)
Sour cream 15% fat 1 table spoon / 15g. (yes)
Pepper (ground) 1 pinch / 0,5g. ()
Nutmeg 1 pinch / 0,5g. (yes)
Lemon juice 1 teaspoon / 2g. ()
Parsley 2 table spoons / 20g. (rec.)
Salt 1 pinch / 1g. (little)

Cooking instructions:
Wash and peel the asparagus.
Heat water, a little lemon juice and pinch of salt till it boils. Tie the asparagus spears together.
Add the asparagus peel to the cooking water and bring to the boil.
Add the asparagus and cook on low heat for about 20 minutes.
Then remove the asparagus bunches and pour the broth through a sieve.
For the roux, heat the oil in a saucepan, add the flour and sauté until it is colorless, slowly top up with the asparagus sauce and simmer for 10 minutes. Cut the asparagus spears into pieces about 3 cm long and place them to the soup.

Just before serving, bring the soup to the boil again.
Mix the egg yolk with the milk and sour cream.
Remove the pot from the heat and stir in the egg yolk and milk mixture.
Season with pepper and nutmeg, decorate with the chopped parsley and serve immediately.

9.3 Banana Soymilk

Good to fight loss of appetite, oral mucosa inflammation. Strengthens body energy, promotes stomach-spleen harmony, promotes digestion, regulates gastrointestinal function. Relieves pain, detoxifying, bactericide.
Cooking time approx. 5 min
Allergens: E
2 portions to 263g. / 126kcal. - (carb:60% / prot:40%)
100g.=47,72kcal. / protein 7,49g. fat:4,13g.
µg. - Ph:10,97 Na:125,56 Ka:55,04 Mg:6,65 Ca:4,89 Fe:0,2 Zn:0,11 Col.:0 Hsr.:16,84

Quantity of ingredients:
Banana 1 piece / 120g. (rec.)
Soybean milk 1 1/2 cups / 400g. (little)
Honey 1 teaspoon / 3g. (little)
Cinnamon ground 1 pinch / 1g. (yes)
Acerola fruit nectar or powder 1 teaspoon / 2g. (little)

Cooking instructions:
Cut the banana into pieces, puree them with soy milk, acerola, honey and cinnamon with the mixing stick.

9.4 Barley mash with berries

Diuretic, forcing spleen, supports urination, laxative, strengthens kidney, promotes digestion, detoxifying, promotes perspiration, reduces blood lipids, stimulates, dissolves stagnation.
Cooking time approx. 2 hours
Allergens: A
5 portions to 318,6g. / 113kcal. - (carb:82% / prot:18%)
100g.=35,34kcal. / protein 4,01g. fat:0,78g.
µg. - Ph:1,47 Na:0,11 Ka:2,69 Mg:0,63 Ca:0,55 Fe:0,02 Zn:0,01 Col.:0 Hsr.:0,48

Quantity of ingredients:
Water 10 cups / 1200g. (yes)
Barley 1 cup / 120g. (yes)
Ginger fresh 2 slices / 2g. ()
Cardamom 3 capsules / 1g. (yes)
Salt 1 pinch / 1g. (little)
Raspberry 5/8 lbs - 8oz / 250g. (yes)
Cocoa 1 pinch / 1g. (little)
Barley malt 1 table spoon / 15g. (yes)
Lemon Balm (fresh) 2-4 leaves / 3g. (yes)

Cooking instructions:
Boil the barley with water, ginger and cardamom pods in a large saucepan. Close pot with a lid and cook over low heat for about 2 hours.

For 2 servings of cooked barley porridge, place about 2 ladles in a bowl. Stir with sunflower seeds, malt, cocoa powder and a pinch of salt. Stir fresh berries into the porridge and serve sprinkled with fresh mint or lemon balm.

Tip: The pre-cooked barley porridge (without fruit) can be stored well in the refrigerator and used for sweet or savory dishes, e.g. with stewed vegetables or fruit seasoned compote.

9.5 Basic recipe for a beef broth (clear)

Strengthens muscles, tendons and bones, reduces blood pressure, strengthens immune system, prevents cancer, reduces radiation damage, stimulates digestion, reduces pain, promotes digestion, diuretic. Rosemary stimulates digestion.
Cooking time approx. 4-8 hours
Allergens: O
10 portions to 276g. / 114kcal. - (carb:22% / prot:78%)
100g.=41,41kcal. / protein 12,22g. fat:4,09g.
µg. - Ph:0,51 Na:0,31 Ka:1,34 Mg:0,11 Ca:0,25 Fe:0,01 Zn:0,01 Col.:0,14 Hsr.:0,36

Quantity of ingredients:
Beef soup meat 1,1 lbs / 500g. (little)
Beef meatbones 5/8 oz / 200g. (little)
Vinegar (Red wine vinegar) 1 dash / 3g. (little)
Juniper berry 8 pieces / 6g. (yes)
Rosemary 1 pinch / 1g. (yes)
Carrot 3 pieces / 210g. (rec.)
Parsnip 2 pieces / 300g. (yes)
Leek 1 piece / 200g. ()
Ginger fresh 1/2 teaspoon / 5g. ()
Lovage 1 stem / 15g. (rec.)
Clove 2 pieces / 2g. (yes)
Pimento 6 pieces / 12g. (yes)
Anise (Common Fennel) 2 pieces / 1g. (rec.)
Salt 1 teaspoon / 5g. (little)
Water 3,3 lbs / 1300g. (yes)

Cooking instructions:
Heat water, a dash of red wine vinegar, some juniper berries, a little rosemary, bones and meat till it boils; add carrot, parsnip, leek, ginger, lovage, clove, allspice, star anise and a little salt; simmer for 4-8 hours then strain.
Refrigerate for later use.

9.6 Basic recipe for a chicken broth worming

Strengthens blood, strengthens bone marrow, reduces blood pressure, strengthens immune system, prevents cancer, reduces radiation damage, promotes sweating, dissolves stagnation, good to fight loss of appetite, flatulence.
Cooking time approx. 2-3 hours
Allergens: L
9 portions to 244,89g. / 90kcal. - (carb:10% / prot:90%)
100g.=36,66kcal. / protein 15,68g. fat:11,56g.
µg. - Ph:0,86 Na:0,59 Ka:1,87 Mg:0,13 Ca:0,38 Fe:0,01 Zn:0 Col.:0,25 Hsr.:0,92

Quantity of ingredients:
Chicken meat 1/2 piece / 600g. (little)
Carrot 2 pieces / 150g. (rec.)
Leek 1 stick / 45g. ()
Celery root 1 piece / 500g. (rec.)
Ginger fresh 2 slices / 2g. ()
Juniper berry 1 teaspoon / 3g. (yes)
Bay leaf 3 pieces / 2g. (yes)
Water 4 cup / 900g. (yes)

Cooking instructions:
Remove chicken parts from fat. Place chicken pieces in a saucepan with hot water and heat till it boils briefly, skimming any resulting foam. Add coarsely chopped vegetables and all spices and cook over medium heat for 2 to 3 hours. Strain the finished soup. Throw away vegetables and bones.
Tip: If you want to use the meat as a soup insert, take out after 45 minutes and return only the bones in the soup.
Refrigerate for later use.

9.7 Basic recipe for a reissue soup (Congee)

Low fat content, for the drainage of the body overweight and high blood pressure.
Cooking time approx. 2-4 hours
3 portions to 273,33g. / 140kcal. - (carb:90% / prot:10%)
100g.=51,34kcal. / protein 2,96g. fat:0,48g.
µg. - Ph:1,95 Na:0,19 Ka:1,67 Mg:1,14 Ca:0,57 Fe:0,01 Zn:0,02 Col.:0 Hsr.:2,11

Quantity of ingredients:
Rice variety any 1 cup / 120g. (yes)
Water 6 cups / 700g. (yes)

Cooking instructions:
Cook rice and water in a ratio of about 1: 6. The amount of water determines the thickness of the mash (matter of taste).
Put the rice in a saucepan with a heavy lid. It is important to simmer the rice after a short boil on the slightest flame, otherwise it burns.
Boil the rice for 2-4 hours. The longer he cooks, the more he strengthens.
If you want to eat the dish for breakfast, you can put the rice on just before bedtime.
To be on the safe side, you should first check the behavior of your pot and cooker under observation for a similar amount of time, so that nothing burns.
Refrigerate for later use.

9.8   Basic recipe for a vegetable soup, nutritious

Reduces blood pressure, strengthens immune system, prevents cancer, forcing spleen, dissolves stagnation, promotes weight loss. Good to fight immunodeficiency, high blood pressure, depressions, diabetes, diarrhea, reduces blood lipids.
Cooking time approx. 2-3 hours
Allergens: L
5 portions to 240,6g. / 48kcal. - (carb:71% / prot:29%)
100g.=19,87kcal. / protein 1,56g. fat:1,31g.
µg. - Ph:0,97 Na:0,73 Ka:5,14 Mg:0,36 Ca:1,26 Fe:0,02 Zn:0,01 Col.:0 Hsr.:0,56

Quantity of ingredients:
Olive oil 1 table spoon / 4g. (little)
Onion white 1 piece / 60g. ()
Carrot 3 pieces / 200g. (rec.)
Parsnip 3/8 lbs - 6oz / 150g. (yes)
Celery root 1 cup / 100g. (rec.)
Ginger fresh 1/2 teaspoon / 2g. ()
Lemon 1/2 piece / 25g. ()
Juniper berry 6 pieces / 6g. (yes)
Thyme dried 1 pinch / 1g. (yes)
Lovage 1 table spoon / 3g. (rec.)
Bay leaf 2 leaves / 1g. (yes)
Salt 1 pinch / 1g. (little)
Water 3 cups / 650g. (yes)

Cooking instructions:
Cut the vegetables into cubes.
Heat oil in hot pot, fry shortly onions and vegetables.
Add cold water, then add ginger, bay leaf and lemon juice.
Season with juniper, thyme and lovage. Cover for 2 - 3 hours on a low heat and simmer.
The used vegetables should be thrown away.
The basic recipe serves as a soup base and to refine vegetables, legumes or cereals.
If you want to eat vegetable soup immediately, add the desired vegetables half an hour before.
Refrigerate for later use.

9.9 Black root with yogurt

Stimulates kidney, bladder and forces the cleaning of the body. In the physiological sense, they generally stimulate the glands in the organism. Good to fight acute or chronic constipation of the intestine. Rich in Vitamins and trace elements.
Cooking time approx. 20 min
Allergens: AG

2 portions to 304,5g. / 319kcal. - (carb:77% / prot:23%)
100g.=104,76kcal. / protein 7,98g. fat:2,08g.
µg. - Ph:22,7 Na:23,23 Ka:67,95 Mg:6,53 Ca:15,06 Fe:0,64 Zn:0,11 Col.:0,16 Hsr.:14,42

Quantity of ingredients:
Salsify 1 lbs / 400g. (yes)
Yogurt (natural, 1.5% fat) 4 table spoons / 80g. (yes)
Salt 1 pinch / 1g. (little)
Multi-grain bread (gray bread) 6 slices / 120g. (little)
Herbs various 1 handful / 5g. (yes)

Cooking instructions:
Peel the salsify and simmer in salted water until tender. Pour away the water, cool the salsify and cut it to size. Cover with yoghurt and sprinkle with fresh herbs. Serve with the bread.
You can also use the salsify from the conserve.

9.10 Blueberry puree

Bilberry is laxative. Clove dissolves stagnation. Cinnamon powder heats stomach and spleen, improves blood circulation.
Cooking time approx. 10 min
1 portion to 271g. / 10kcal. - (carb:78% / prot:22%)
100g.=3,69kcal. / protein 0,2g. fat:0,32g.
µg. - Ph:0,98 Na:1 Ka:5,56 Mg:1,09 Ca:6 Fe:0,06 Zn:0,1 Col.:0 Hsr.:1,48

Quantity of ingredients:
Blueberry 1/2 oz / 20g. (yes)
Cinnamon ground 1 pinch / 0,1g. (yes)
Clove 1 piece / 1g. (yes)
Water 1 cup / 250g. (yes)

Cooking instructions:
Boil blueberries with cinnamon and clove in water for 10 minutes. Remove the cinnamon and clove. Puree. Sweet as desired.

9.11 Carrot and rice gruel soup

Stops diarrhea, good to fight fever, strengthens immune system, reduces blood pressure.
Cooking time approx. 10 min
1 portion to 224g. / 101kcal. - (carb:96% / prot:4%)
100g.=45,09kcal. / protein 2,37g. fat:0,4g.
µg. - Ph:27,48 Na:20,34 Ka:65,63 Mg:170,89 Ca:178,57 Fe:1,03 Zn:0,34 Col.:0 Hsr.:12,3

Quantity of ingredients:
Basic recipe for a rice soup (Congee) 1 cup / 120g. (rec.)
Carrot 2 pieces / 100g. (rec.)
Salt 1 teaspoon / 4g. (little)

Cooking instructions:
Peel and grate carrots. Heat the rice soup (according to the basic recipe) till it boils and add the grated carrots and salt. Cook for 10 minutes.

9.12 Carrots with potato foam

Promotes spleen and liver, reduces blood pressure, strengthens immune system. Improves digestion, regenerates skin, supports urination, lowers cholesterol, promotes the production of stool and urine, strengthens blood, strengthens nerves.
Cooking time approx. 30 min
Allergens: G

1 portion to 322g. / 316kcal. - (carb:21% / prot:79%)
100g.=98,14kcal. / protein 11,65g. fat:15,45g.
µg. - Ph:48,48 Na:21,61 Ka:208,2 Mg:18,25 Ca:23,85 Fe:1,22 Zn:0,5 Col.:15,53 Hsr.:26,24

Quantity of ingredients:
Carrot (Early Carrot) 3/8 lbs - 6oz / 150g. (rec.)
Pork meat 1/8 lbs - 2oz / 40g. (little)
Potato (mealy) 1/4 lbs - 4oz / 100g. (rec.)
Butter organic 1 table spoon / 10g. (yes)
Honey 1/2 teaspoon / 2g. (little)
Anise (Common Fennel) 1 pinch / 0,2g. (rec.)
Water 2 table spoons / 20g. (yes)

Cooking instructions:
Clean the carrots, wash thoroughly, peel thinly and cut into thin slices. Cut the meat into strips.
Wash the potatoes, cook in a small saucepan with little water in about 15 minutes.
Melt half of the butter in a saucepan, fry the carrots and the meat in it. If necessary, add 2-3 tablespoons of water, put the lid on and cook everything over low heat in about 15 minutes.
Add the honey, the anise and the remaining butter and remove the pot from the heat.
Peel the potatoes and press directly onto the plate with the potato press. Distribute the honey carrots over it.

9.13 Celery soup

Forcing spleen, calms nerves, stimulates appetite and digestion, dissolves stagnation.
Cooking time approx. 45 min
Allergens: ACGL

4 portions to 285,5g. / 101kcal. - (carb:44% / prot:56%)
100g.=35,38kcal. / protein 4,32g. fat:5,7g.
µg. - Ph:2,76 Na:5,05 Ka:11,06 Mg:0,62 Ca:2,85 Fe:0,03 Zn:0,01 Col.:1,44 Hsr.:2,12

Quantity of ingredients:
Water 2 cup / 500g. (yes)
Butter organic 1 table spoon / 15g. (yes)
Nutmeg 1 pinch / 1g. (yes)
Salt 1 pinch / 1g. (little)
Spelled wholemeal flour 2-3 teaspoons / 25g. (little)
Celery root 1 piece / 500g. (rec.)
Chicken egg 1 piece / 55g. (little)
Cream sour 10% 2 table spoons / 25g. (yes)
Celery sticks 2 table spoons / 20g. (yes)
Pepper (ground) 1 pinch / 0,5g. ()

Cooking instructions:
In a hot saucepan, melt 1 tbsp butter; add a pinch of nutmeg, a pinch of salt, 1/2 cup wholegrain spelled flour (finely ground as fresh as possible) and stir to a sweat while stirring; add 1/2 liter of hot water gradually; add 1 large finely chopped celery tuber; cook for about 35 minutes and then puree; mix 1 egg yolk with 1 cup of cream; in the hot - no longer boiling! - soup vigorously; add some celery leaves finely chopped; with pepper, salt to taste.

9.14 Chicken soup with egg yolk and parsley

Strengthens blood, strengthens bone marrow, reduces blood pressure, strengthens immune system. Parsley stimulates liver function, harmonizes liver and spleen, strengthens eyesight, detoxifying.
Cooking time approx. 10 min
Allergens: CL
2 portions to 260g. / 118kcal. - (carb:82% / prot:18%)
100g.=45,19kcal. / protein 16,35g. fat:2,49g.
µg. - Ph:6,98 Na:8,83 Ka:9 Mg:24,79 Ca:69,4 Fe:0,28 Zn:0,05 Col.:6,52 Hsr.:2,22

Quantity of ingredients:
Basic recipe for a chicken soup (warming) 2 cup / 500g. (rec.)
Chicken yolk 1 piece / 10g. (little)
Parsley 1 table spoon / 10g. (rec.)

Cooking instructions:
Cook the chicken broth according to the basic recipe.
Heat broth and bubble the egg yolk. Sprinkle the chopped parsley over it and let it rest for about 2 minutes. Drink in small sips.

9.15 Compote from apples

Apple (sweet) stops diarrhea, promotes digestion, appetizing, harmonizes the stomach. Warms stomach and spleen, improves blood circulation.
Cooking time approx. 10 min
2 portions to 220,5g. / 67kcal. - (carb:96% / prot:4%)
100g.=30,39kcal. / protein 0,24g. fat:0,45g.
µg. - Ph:1,41 Na:0,51 Ka:18,22 Mg:0,9 Ca:2,16 Fe:0,07 Zn:0,02 Col.:0 Hsr.:1,87

Quantity of ingredients:
Apple (sweet) 1 piece / 220g. (little)
Water 1 1/2 cups / 220g. (yes)
Cinnamon ground 1 pinch / 1g. (yes)

Cooking instructions:
Cook the apples (organic) with the skin and seeds. Sprinkle with cinnamon.

9.16 Compote from rhubarb

Antipyretic, analgesic, detoxifying, bactericide.
Cooking time approx. 15 min
1 portion to 230g. / 48kcal. - (carb:92% / prot:8%)
100g.=20,87kcal. / protein 0,64g. fat:0,1g.
µg. - Ph:11,22 Na:1,7 Ka:119,43 Mg:6,43 Ca:25,43 Fe:0,28 Zn:0,15 Col.:0 Hsr.:2,61

Quantity of ingredients:
Rhubarb 1/4 lbs - 4oz / 100g. (yes)
Water 1 cup / 120g. (yes)
Honey 1 table spoon / 10g. (little)

Cooking instructions:
Wash rhubarb and cut small. Boil in the water. Allow to cool a little and add the honey.

9.17 Corn coffee with cardamom

Diuretic, forcing spleen, supports urination, relaxes, reduces fat.
Cooking time approx. 5 min
1 portion to 136g. / 3kcal. - (carb:99% / prot:1%)
100g.=2,21kcal. / protein 0,11g. fat:0,08g.
µg. - Ph:1,29 Na:1,02 Ka:7,9 Mg:2,49 Ca:5,37 Fe:0,08 Zn:0,09 Col.:0 Hsr.:0

Quantity of ingredients:
Cereal coffee 1 table spoon / 15g. (yes)
Cardamom 2 cores / 1g. (yes)
Water 1 cup / 120g. (yes)

Cooking instructions:
Boil water, coffee, sugar and cardamom. Let it set for one min before drinking.

9.18 Cottage cheese with steamed fruit

Good to fight loss of appetite, promotes digestion, supports urination.
Cooking time approx. 20 min
Allergens: G
2 portions to 250g. / 214kcal. - (carb:40% / prot:60%)
100g.=85,8kcal. / protein 18,45g. fat:6,4g.
μg. - Ph:22,3 Na:57,25 Ka:25,45 Mg:1,85 Ca:12,8 Fe:0,05 Zn:0,09 Col.:0,64 Hsr.:1,5

Quantity of ingredients:
Cottage cheese 3/4 lbs / 300g. (rec.)
Apple (sour) 1 piece / 100g. (little)
Pear 1 piece / 100g. (little)

Cooking instructions:
Wash apples and pears well, do not peel, and chop small. In a pot with steam filter, boil them al dente, remove and allow to cool down.
Serve the cheese, spread the fruit on it.

9.19 Cranberry juice

Antibacterial, good to fight loss of appetite, arteriosclerosis, bladder infections, diarrhea, colds. Antipyretic, against free radicals, gout, diuretic, stomach ulcers, oral mucosa inflammation, rheumatism.
Cooking time approx. 5 min
1 portion to 160g. / 43kcal. - (carb:98% / prot:2%)
100g.=26,88kcal. / protein 0,14g. fat:0,02g.
μg. - Ph:2,06 Na:1,53 Ka:11,69 Mg:1,16 Ca:4,22 Fe:0,09 Zn:0,09 Col.:0 Hsr.:3,12

Quantity of ingredients:
Cranberries 2 table spoons / 25g. (little)
Water 1 cup / 125g. (yes)
Honey 1 table spoon / 10g. (little)

Cooking instructions:
Mix the cranberries with a little water with the blender to a pulp. Add the remaining water and sweeten with the honey.

9.20 Cranberry yogurt mix

Good to fight acute or chronic constipation of the intestine, oral mucosal inflammation, diarrhea, flatulence, throat irritation.
Cooking time approx. 5 min
Allergens: GO
2 portions to 197,5g. / 57kcal. - (carb:75% / prot:25%)
100g.=28,86kcal. / protein 2,13g. fat:1,02g.
µg. - Ph:7,17 Na:5,87 Ka:13,16 Mg:2,71 Ca:16,61 Fe:0,01 Zn:0,03 Col.:0,39 Hsr.:0,2

Quantity of ingredients:
Yogurt (natural, 1.5% fat) 1/4 lbs - 4oz / 125g. (yes)
Cranberry jam 2 table spoons / 20g. (yes)
Mineral water 1 cup / 250g. (yes)

Cooking instructions:
Mix yoghurt, cranberry jam and mineral water until frothy.

9.21 Fennel and potato gratin

Reduces inflammation, improves blood circulation, improves digestion, supports urination, lowers cholesterol, good to fight loss of appetite, flatulence, inflammatory bowel disease, heartburn. Forcing spleen, improves blood circulation.
Cooking time approx. 1 1/2 hours
Allergens: CGL
2 portions to 230,5g. / 147kcal. - (carb:68% / prot:32%)
100g.=63,77kcal. / protein 5,72g. fat:5,42g.
µg. - Ph:15 Na:12,98 Ka:80,91 Mg:13,52 Ca:40,41 Fe:0,41 Zn:0,09 Col.:7,81 Hsr.:3,64

Quantity of ingredients:
Fennel 5/8 oz / 200g. (rec.)
Potato 1/4 lbs - 4oz / 125g. (rec.)
Basic recipe for a vegetable soup (nutritious) 1/2 cup / 100g. (rec.)
Butter organic 1 teaspoon / 3g. (yes)
Rice flour 2 teaspoons / 6g. (yes)
Cream sour 10% 1 teaspoon / 3g. (yes)
Salt 1 pinch / 1g. (little)
Sugar cane sugar 1 pinch / 1g. (little)
Chicken yolk 1 piece / 10g. (little)
Pepper Cayenne 1 pinch / 0,5g. ()

Nutmeg 1 pinch / 0,5g. (yes)
Parsley 1 teaspoon / 2g. (rec.)
Chives 1 teaspoon / 3g. ()
Parmesan 1 teaspoon / 3g. ()
Butter organic 1 teaspoon / 3g. (yes)

Cooking instructions:
Cook peeled potatoes and then let cool. Wash the fennel, cut off the stems and remove any outer leaves.
Hold back fennel greens and add it to the sauce with the other herbs later.
Steam the fennel tubers for about 15 - 20 minutes.
Then cut the potatoes and fennel into slices and place in layers in a greased baking dish.
Bring the liquid of fennel broth to the boil and bind it with flour.
Season with sea salt, cayenne pepper, sugar, nutmeg and sour cream.
Allow to cool and alloy with egg yolk.
Spread the sauce over the casserole, sprinkle with parmesan and finely chopped parsley and chives. Bake at 200 °C / 392 °F in the oven for half an hour.

9.22 Frozen pineapple juice

Pineapple reduce inflammation, supports urination, cleans the skin.
Cooking time approx. 1 1/2 hours
1 portion to 50g. / 29kcal. - (carb:95% / prot:5%)
100g.=58kcal. / protein 0,25g. fat:0,1g.
µg. - Ph:9 Na:2 Ka:173 Mg:17 Ca:16 Fe:0,4 Zn:0,3 Col.:0 Hsr.:7

Quantity of ingredients:
Pineapple 1/8 lbs - 2oz / 50g. (little)

Cooking instructions:
Juice pineapple yourself or freeze the organic pineapple juice in small portions and if necessary suck.

9.23 Grated apple

Eat 3 times a day - Apple (sour) scraped and brown is stuffing. Relieves diarrhea.
Cooking time approx. 10 min
1 portion to 200g. / 120kcal. - (carb:94% / prot:6%)
100g.=60kcal. / protein 0,6g. fat:0,8g.
µg. - Ph:11 Na:3 Ka:144 Mg:6 Ca:7 Fe:0,5 Zn:0,1 Col.:0 Hsr.:15

Quantity of ingredients:
Apple (sour) 1 piece / 200g. (little)

Cooking instructions:
Peel apple and grate as fine as possible. Leave for at least 5 minutes until it turns brown.

9.24 Kohlrabi in chervil sauce with potatoes

Reduces inflammation, lowers cholesterol, diuretic, conducts bowel winds, strengthens immune system, prevents cancer, promotes weight loss. Good to fight loss of appetite, flatulence, high blood pressure, depressions, diabetes, diarrhea.
Cooking time approx. 1 hour
Allergens: GL
4 portions to 316,75g. / 188kcal. - (carb:79% / prot:21%)
100g.=59,19kcal. / protein 8,66g. fat:2,51g.
µg. - Ph:2,95 Na:1,03 Ka:25,06 Mg:3,48 Ca:15,16 Fe:0,04 Zn:0,02 Col.:0,06 Hsr.:0,91

Quantity of ingredients:
Potato 6 pieces / 450g. (rec.)
Basic recipe for a vegetable soup (nutritious) 1 cup / 300g. (rec.)
Potato 1/4 lbs - 4oz / 100g. (rec.)
Nutmeg 1 pinch / 0,2g. (yes)
Lemon peel 1/2 teaspoon / 2g. ()
Ginger fresh 1/2 teaspoon / 2g. ()
Lovage 1/2 teaspoon / 2g. (rec.)
Kohlrabi 3/4 lbs / 300g. (yes)
Salt 1 pinch / 1g. (little)
Pepper (ground) 1 pinch / 0,2g. ()
Sour cream 15% fat 3 table spoons / 30g. (yes)
Chervil dried 1 Bunch / 80g. (rec.)

Cooking instructions:
Boil the potatoes in salted water.
Bring half of the vegetable stock to boil. Add the diced potatoes, nutmeg, lemon zest, ginger and lovage. Cover the potatoes and cook for about 10 minutes until soft and puree them with a blender until they are smooth.
Bring remaining vegetable stock to boil. Cut kohlrabi into cubes and add, cover and cook for about 8 minutes. Stir in the potato sauce and heat everything briefly. Puree with the mixing stick chervil and sour cream. Mix the chervil cream with the kohlrabi vegetables.
Serve with the cooked, peeled potatoes.

9.25 Kohlrabi Potatoes mash

Diuretic, harmonizes the stomach and intestines, conducts bowel winds. Improves digestion, regenerates skin, supports urination, lowers cholesterol.
Cooking time approx. 25 min
Allergens: CG
1 portion to 285g. / 278kcal. - (carb:47% / prot:53%)
100g.=97,54kcal. / protein 9,09g. fat:16,54g.
µg. - Ph:95,3 Na:22,19 Ka:332,32 Mg:30,81 Ca:50,63 Fe:1,25 Zn:0,6 Col.:118,95 Hsr.:21,58

Quantity of ingredients:
Kohlrabi 1/2 piece / 150g. (yes)
Potato 1/4 lbs - 4oz / 100g. (rec.)
Butter organic 1 table spoon / 10g. (yes)
Chicken yolk 1 piece / 25g. (little)

Cooking instructions:
Remove the kohlrabi leaves, wash the tuber and tender leaves and the potatoes thoroughly. Peel the kohlrabi and potatoes, cut into cubes about 1 cm in size. Melt half the butter in a small saucepan, add the kohlrabi and the potatoes and fry in it. Steam with 2 tablespoons of water in a closed saucepan over low heat for about 15 minutes. Meanwhile, free the tenderest kohlrabi leaves from the stems and chop very finely. In total, at most 2 tablespoons of leaf pieces should be used. Add this to the vegetables about 5 minutes before the end of the cooking time. Stir in the egg yolk and bring to the boil again. Put the vegetables in a plate and mix with the remaining butter and egg yolk.

9.26 Mango banana yoghurt drink ice cold

Good to fight loss of appetite, oral mucosa inflammation. Regulates gastrointestinal function, chronic constipation. Prevents cancer. Diuretic, forcing spleen.
Cooking time approx. 5 min
Allergens: G
2 portions to 226g. / 121kcal. - (carb:87% / prot:13%)
100g.=53,54kcal. / protein 2,72g. fat:1,05g.
µg. - Ph:7,97 Na:3,73 Ka:51,04 Mg:5,37 Ca:11,04 Fe:0,07 Zn:0,04 Col.:0,28 Hsr.:2,87

Quantity of ingredients:
Mango juice 1/2 cup / 100g. (little)
Yogurt (natural, 1.5% fat) 1/4 lbs - 4oz / 100g. (yes)
Mineral water 1/2 cup / 100g. (yes)
Banana 1/2 piece / 150g. (rec.)
Acerola fruit nectar or powder 1 teaspoon / 2g. (little)

Cooking instructions:
Mix all the ingredients and 2-3 ice cubes in a blender.

9.27 Nettle-chard soup

Nettle promotes urination, detoxifies, supporting prostate disorders, reduces inflammation, analgesic. Chard supports intestinal activity, cleans intestine.
Cooking time approx. 30 min
4 portions to 230,25g. / 52kcal. - (carb:41% / prot:59%)
100g.=22,58kcal. / protein 2,63g. fat:2,86g.
µg. - Ph:1,42 Na:3,16 Ka:13,09 Mg:2,82 Ca:3,79 Fe:0,09 Zn:0,01 Col.:0 Hsr.:2,45

Quantity of ingredients:
Nettles 1 handful / 10g. (yes)
Chard 1 lbs / 500g. (yes)
Salt 1 pinch / 1g. (little)
Water 2 cup / 400g. (yes)
Olive oil 1 table spoon / 10g. (little)
Pepper (ground) 1 pinch / 0,5g. ()

Cooking instructions:
Heat the oil in a saucepan, add the washed and finely chopped Swiss chard. Salt and let simmer for 10 minutes. Add the chopped nettles and cook for another 10 minutes. Add pepper and puree.

9.28 Noodle soup - Also for babies from 10 month

Protects the digestive system. Detoxifying, affects anorexia, reduces blood pressure, strengthens immune system, strengthens the muscles, tendons and bones. stimulates liver function, detoxifying.
Cooking time approx. 1 1/2 hours
Allergens: ACEGL
8 portions to 303,88g. / 237kcal. - (carb:64% / prot:36%)
100g.=77,91kcal. / protein 14,74g. fat:5,04g.
µg. - Ph:1,07 Na:0,71 Ka:2,97 Mg:0,29 Ca:0,49 Fe:0,02 Zn:0,02 Col.:0,34 Hsr.:0,89

Quantity of ingredients:
Beef soup meat 3/4 lbs / 300g. (little)
Water 4 cup / 900g. (yes)
Bay leaf 1 piece / 1g. (yes)
Carrot 3/4 lbs / 300g. (rec.)
Celery sticks 1 bunch / 200g. (yes)
Cauliflower 3/4 lbs / 300g. (little)
Parsley 1 Bunch / 100g. (rec.)
Noodles (wheat) with egg 3/4 lbs / 300g. (yes)
Butter organic 1 table spoon / 10g. (yes)
Salt 1 teaspoon / 2g. (little)
Soy sauce 1 table spoon / 8g. (little)
Tomato paste 1 table spoon / 10g. (little)

Cooking instructions:
Simmer the meat and bay leaf in the water over low heat for about 30 minutes. Peel and slice the carrots. From the celery plant separate the lower end and the leaves. Wash the stems, peel off the tough threads and cut the stems into slices about 1 cm thick.
Wash the Brussels sprouts, clean them and cut the roses from below crosswise.
Wash and chop the parsley.

Add the Brussels sprouts and carrot slices to the soup and cook for about 30 minutes.

After about 10 minutes, add the celery and green leaves and the pasta. Finally, remove the bay leaf and celery green.

(For the baby, remove about 200-250 g of carrots, celery and noodles with broth, squeeze about 35 g of meat finely and add to the baby soup, stir in the butter and 1 teaspoon of chopped parsley.)

Season the remaining soup with the salt, the soy sauce, the tomato paste and the remaining parsley. Lift out the meat. Remove fat and bones and dice the meat. Serve in the soup.

9.29 Oat Congee

Strengthens immune system.
Cooking time approx. 2-4 hours
Allergens: A
3 portions to 275g. / 162kcal. - (carb:74% / prot:26%)
100g.=58,91kcal. / protein 7,04g. fat:2,87g.
µg. - Ph:5,76 Na:0,23 Ka:5,98 Mg:2,27 Ca:1,82 Fe:0,1 Zn:0,08 Col.:0 Hsr.:2,51

Quantity of ingredients:
Oat 1 cup / 125g. (yes)
Water 6 cups / 700g. (yes)

Cooking instructions:
Cook oats and water in a ratio of about 1: 6. The amount of water determines the thickness of the mash (pure matter of taste). The oats swell, so do not take much. Put the oats in a saucepan with good insulation and a heavy lid. It is important to simmer the oats after a short boil on the slightest flame, otherwise it burns. Cook the oat for 2-4 hours. The longer it cooks, the more he strengthens.

9.30 Potato with dandelion salad

Promotes spleen, reduces inflammation, improves digestion, regenerates skin, supports urinating, lowers cholesterol, detoxifying, reduces inflammation, forcing spleen and digestive system, detoxifying, dissolves stagnation.
Cooking time approx. 25 min
2 portions to 203g. / 162kcal. - (carb:70% / prot:30%)
100g.=79,8kcal. / protein 4,28g. fat:5,59g.
µg. - Ph:26,58 Na:13,03 Ka:176,11 Mg:11,88 Ca:27,41 Fe:0,61 Zn:0,28 Col.:0,01 Hsr.:14,22

Quantity of ingredients:
Potato 5/8 lbs - 8oz / 250g. (rec.)
Onion white 1/2 piece / 20g. ()
Sunflower oil 1 table spoon / 10g. (little)
Dandelion (young plants) 1/4 lbs - 4oz / 125g. (yes)
Salt 1 pinch / 1g. (little)
Pepper white (ground) 1 pinch / 0,5g. ()

Cooking instructions:
Cook the potatoes in salted water and cut into thin slices. Finely chop the onion. Now season the potatoes with oil, salt and pepper and add the dandelion and mix.

9.31 Pumpkin soup

Promotes digestion, forcing spleen and stomach, reduces blood pressure, strengthens immune system, prevents cancer, reduces radiation damage, improves digestion, regenerates skin, lowers cholesterol, reduces blood glucose, protects liver.
Cooking time approx. 1 hour
3 portions to 236,33g. / 105kcal. - (carb:71% / prot:29%)
100g.=44,29kcal. / protein 2,54g. fat:3,64g.
µg. - Ph:4,02 Na:0,96 Ka:24,72 Mg:1,82 Ca:2,89 Fe:0,08 Zn:0,02 Col.:0 Hsr.:1,08

Quantity of ingredients:
Pumpkin 3/4 lbs / 300g. (rec.)
Carrot 2 pieces / 100g. (rec.)
Potato 2 pieces / 120g. (rec.)
Olive oil 1 table spoon / 10g. (little)
Onion white 1 piece / 50g. ()
Water 1 cup / 120g. (yes)
Parsley 1 table spoon / 7g. (rec.)
Anise (Common Fennel) 1 pinch / 1g. (rec.)
Salt 1 pinch / 1g. (little)

Cooking instructions:
Add the olive oil to the pan, add the diced pumpkin, diced carrots and potatoes. Roast them shortly, add the finely chopped onion, fill with water, add enough water to cover the vegetables at least 3 finger-widths. Boil at low heat.

Season with sea salt, add small cutted parsley, a pinch of anise (little). Allow to simmer for about 35 minutes. Then purée the soup and add some water, depending on the consistency of the soup.

9.32 Pumpkin-yoghurt soup

Relaxes, reduces blood pressure, strengthens immune system, promotes weight loss. Good to fight immunodeficiency, loss of appetite, flatulence, depressions, diabetes, diarrhea.
Cooking time approx. 15 min
Allergens: GL
4 portions to 239g. / 68kcal. - (carb:83% / prot:17%)
100g.=28,45kcal. / protein 2,37g. fat:1,31g.
µg. - Ph:1,79 Na:0,9 Ka:6,6 Mg:2,8 Ca:10,96 Fe:0,02 Zn:0,01 Col.:0,05 Hsr.:0,35

Quantity of ingredients:
Basic recipe for a vegetable soup (nutritious) 1 cup / 300g. (rec.)
Hokkaido pumpkin 1,1 lbs / 500g. (rec.)
Ginger fresh 1/2 teaspoon / 2g. ()
Fennel seeds ground 1/2 teaspoon / 1g. (rec.)
Anise (Common Fennel) 1/4 teaspoon / 1g. (rec.)
Yogurt (natural, 1.5% fat) 3/8 lbs - 6oz / 150g. (yes)
Peppermint 2 leaves / 1g. (yes)
Salt 1 pinch / 1g. (little)

Cooking instructions:
Heat the vegetable broth (after the basic recipe) till it boils. Add diced pumpkin, chopped ginger, crushed fennel seeds and anise. Bring the soup to the boil and simmer for about 12 minutes until the pumpkin is soft.
Remove soup from the heat. Puree the soup with the yoghurt with the blender. Serve soup with finely chopped mint sprinkled.

9.33 Puréed banana

Eat 2 times a day, regulates gastrointestinal function
Cooking time approx. 7 min
1 portion to 150g. / 144kcal. - (carb:95% / prot:5%)
100g.=96kcal. / protein 1,65g. fat:0,3g.
µg. - Ph:28 Na:1 Ka:393 Mg:36 Ca:9 Fe:0,6 Zn:0,2 Col.:0 Hsr.:25

Quantity of ingredients:
Banana 1 piece / 150g. (rec.)

Cooking instructions:
Mix the banana with the fork or purée with a blender. Leave to brown for at least 5 minutes.

9.34 Rhubarb and apple jelly

Antioxidants, lots of vitamin C, laxative, relieves pain, detoxifying, warms stomach and spleen, improves blood circulation.
Cooking time approx. 15 min
2 portions to 276,5g. / 180kcal. - (carb:96% / prot:4%)
100g.=65,1kcal. / protein 1,19g. fat:0,58g.
µg. - Ph:14,75 Na:1,5 Ka:93,5 Mg:7,42 Ca:12,73 Fe:0,29 Zn:0,07 Col.:0 Hsr:6,21

Quantity of ingredients:
Rhubarb 5/8 oz / 200g. (yes)
Apple juice (natural cloudy) 1 cup / 300g. (little)
Corn starch 1 oz / 30g. (yes)
Honey 1/2 oz / 20g. (little)
Vanilla sugar natural 1 pinch / 0,5g. (little)
Cinnamon ground 1 pinch / 0,5g. (yes)
Peppermint 2 leaves / 2g. (yes)

Cooking instructions:
Add the cornstarch to a 1/2 cup apple juice.
Simmer the rhubarb in 1 cup of water for 10 min.
Add the remaining apple juice and the cornstarch, stir, heat till it boils again.
Sweet with honey and season with vanilla and cinnamon. Spread the mixture on dessert bowls and garnish with mint.

9.35 Rice congee with carrots and fennel

Worms, forcing spleen, relieves constipation, stimulates nerves, detoxifying, reduces inflammation, improves blood circulation, reduces blood pressure, strengthens immune system, prevents cancer, reduces radiation damage.
Cooking time approx. 2 hours and more
Allergens: G
3 portions to 284,67g. / 131kcal. - (carb:94% / prot:6%)
100g.=46,14kcal. / protein 4,17g. fat:1,37g.
µg. - Ph:3,26 Na:3,23 Ka:18,37 Mg:21,62 Ca:22,98 Fe:0,13 Zn:0,03 Col.:0,09 Hsr.:1,26

Quantity of ingredients:
Basic recipe for a rice soup (Congee) 2 cup / 500g. (rec.)
Carrot 2 pieces / 100g. (rec.)
Fennel 1 piece / 250g. (rec.)
Butter organic 1 teaspoon / 3g. (yes)
Cardamom 1/2 teaspoon / 1g. (yes)

Cooking instructions:
Cook rice congee according to basic recipe.
Clean and cut carrots and fennel.
When carrots and fennel are cooked from the beginning, they serve wholesomeness. If added shortly before the end of the cooking time, taste and vitamins are retained.

Refine with butter and cardamom before serving.

9.36 Rice with parsnips

Rich in vitamins, minerals potassium and zinc. Good to fight blood circulation disorders, thrombose, risk of embolism, high blood pressure, a headache, heart attack and stroke, yeast infections.
Cooking time approx. 45 min
3 portions to 261,33g. / 206kcal. - (carb:78% / prot:22%)
100g.=78,95kcal. / protein 5,16g. fat:4,52g.
µg. - Ph:6,72 Na:0,7 Ka:31,66 Mg:2,54 Ca:3,53 Fe:0,05 Zn:0,07 Col.:0 Hsr.:4,06

Quantity of ingredients:
Rice variety any 1 cup / 120g. (yes)
Water 1 1/2 cups / 200g. (yes)
Salt 1 pinch / 1g. (little)
Parsnip 3-4 pieces / 450g. (yes)
Olive oil 1 table spoon / 10g. (little)
Sage 1 teaspoon / 3g. (yes)

Cooking instructions:
Peel the parsnips and cut into slices. Fry for a short time in oil. Add the rice and fry again for a short time. Add the water and cook it at least 30 min. Sprinkle with fresh chopped sage.

9.37 Ricepudding

Regulates gastrointestinal function. Strengthens spleen and stomach, strengthens the muscles. Vitamin C rich.
Cooking time approx. 2 hours and more
Allergens: G
1 portion to 329g. / 316kcal. - (carb:76% / prot:24%)
100g.=96,05kcal. / protein 9,26g. fat:7,35g.
µg. - Ph:91,08 Na:31,47 Ka:222,68 Mg:30,22 Ca:77,57 Fe:0,44 Zn:0,42 Col.:3,65 Hsr.:17,51

Quantity of ingredients:
Cow's milk (whole milk 3.5% fat) 3/4 cup - 6 oz / 200g. (little)
Rice round grain 1 oz / 25g. (yes)
Banana 1/4 lbs - 4oz / 100g. (rec.)
Red berry (without sugar) 2 teaspoons / 4g. (yes)

Cooking instructions:
Heat half of the milk till it boils in a small saucepan.
Sprinkle the rice and cook on low heat for about 15 minutes.
Peel the banana, finely grate with the blender and add the beetroot juice.

Mix the banana bran under the hot rice.
Pour a pudding mold (about 1/4 liter of contents) in cold water.
Fill the banana rice in the mold and let the pudding swell at room temperature.
After about 3 hours it is solid and can be toppled.
Take the remaining milk as a drink.

9.38 Roasted millet with Celery sticks

Promotes spleen and kidney, diuretic, promoting metabolism.
Cooking time approx. 30 min
Allergens: L
2 portions to 228g. / 400kcal. - (carb:82% / prot:18%)
100g.=175,44kcal. / protein 7g. fat:2,58g.
µg. - Ph:22,21 Na:4,29 Ka:15,63 Mg:11,94 Ca:5,5 Fe:0,62 Zn:0,24 Col.:0 Hsr.:6,31

Quantity of ingredients:
Millet 1 cup / 120g. (yes)
Water 1 1/2 cups / 240g. (yes)
Celery sticks 2 rods / 50g. (yes)
Herbs various 1 table spoon / 10g. (yes)
Water 2 table spoons / 30g. (yes)
Salt 1 pinch / 1g. (little)
Sage 3-4 leaves / 2g. (yes)
Cress 1 teaspoon / 3g. (rec.)

Cooking instructions:
Roast millet briefly, pour over water, heat till it boils and let stand for 20 min. to swell.

Cut celery into small pieces and mix with water, salt and fresh herbs and cook for 10 min. Add to the millet. Sprinkle fresh sage or watercress over it.

9.39 Rosemary Potatoes

Reduces Inflammation, improves digestion, regenerates skin, supports urination, lowers cholesterol. Rosemary stimulates digestion, strengthens lung, promotes spleen and kidney, dries out.
Cooking time approx. 30 min
2 portions to 216,5g. / 188kcal. - (carb:76% / prot:24%)
100g.=87,07kcal. / protein 4,21g. fat:5,25g.
µg. - Ph:11,51 Na:0,72 Ka:82,88 Mg:4,72 Ca:1,86 Fe:0,1 Zn:0,07 Col.:0 Hsr.:3,64

Quantity of ingredients:
Potato 6-8 pieces / 420g. (rec.)
Salt (herbal) 1 pinch / 1g. (little)
Olive oil 1 table spoon / 10g. (little)
Rosemary 1 teaspoon / 2g. (yes)

Cooking instructions:
Cut the potatoes into half's, apply a little olive oil on the cut surface, then salt, sprinkle 2 - 3 rosemary needles on the potatoes.
Place the potatoes on the baking tray and bake them in the preheated oven for approx. 25 minutes to 190°C/374°F.

9.40 Semolina porridge with banana

Regulates gastrointestinal function, reduces inflammation, antiallergic, good to fight blood circulation disorders.
Cooking time approx. 15 min
Allergens: AG
1 portion to 284g. / 307kcal. - (carb:66% / prot:34%)
100g.=108,1kcal. / protein 10,57g. fat:10,72g.
µg. - Ph:116,7 Na:93,56 Ka:218,89 Mg:28,56 Ca:92,08 Fe:0,64 Zn:0,36 Col.:7,61 Hsr.:12,85

Quantity of ingredients:
Cow's milk (whole milk 3.5% fat) 3/4 cup - 6 oz / 200g. (little)
Spelled semolina 3 table spoons / 30g. (yes)
Butter organic 1 teaspoon / 4g. (yes)
Banana 1/2 piece / 50g. (rec.)

Cooking instructions:
Heat the half of the milk in a small pot. Add the semolina and boil it shortly in the milk. Let it swell at low heat for 3 minutes with constant stirring. Remove the pot from the heat, add the remaining milk with the snow bean and place the mush in a small bowl. Add the butter and the battered banana.
For adults, a pinch of cinnamon can be spread over it.

9.41 Soup with egg yolk

Strengthens muscles, tendons and bones, reduces blood pressure, strengthens immune system.
Cooking time approx. 5 min
Allergens: CO
1 portion to 275g. / 173kcal. - (carb:79% / prot:21%)
100g.=62,91kcal. / protein 13,95g. fat:11,42g.
µg. - Ph:95,65 Na:29,33 Ka:23,55 Mg:84,18 Ca:199,09 Fe:1,38 Zn:1,25 Col.:115,67 Hsr.:3,82

Quantity of ingredients:
Basic recipe for a beef soup (warming) 1 cup / 250g. (rec.)
Chicken yolk 1 piece / 25g. (little)

Cooking instructions:
Warm the beef soup according to the basic recipe for a beef broth, warm it up and jell the yolk.

9.42 Tea from peppermint with white sugar

Peppermint relaxes, frees lungs and nose (inhaling), regulates cycle, detoxifying.
Cooking time approx. 15 min
2 portions to 255g. / 8kcal. - (carb:91% / prot:9%)
100g.=2,94kcal. / protein 0,13g. fat:0,02g.
µg. - Ph:0,24 Na:0,3 Ka:0,92 Mg:0,35 Ca:1,97 Fe:0,01 Zn:0,02 Col.:0 Hsr.:0

Quantity of ingredients:
Peppermint 1 table spoon / 7g. (yes)
Water 2 cup / 500g. (yes)
Sugar candy white 1 teaspoon / 3g. (little)

Cooking instructions:
Heat the water till it boils and put it aside. Add peppermint and 10 min. to let go. Strain. Sweet to taste with honey.

9.43 Tea Green tea

Green tea promotes digestion, supports urination, dissolves mucus, detoxifying, stimulates nerves, reduces blood lipids, lowers cholesterol, reduces inflammation.
Cooking time approx. 10 min
1 portion to 122g. / 2kcal. - (carb:20% / prot:80%)
100g.=1,64kcal. / protein 0g. fat:0g.
µg. - Ph:5,61 Na:1,07 Ka:27,59 Mg:4,07 Ca:9,43 Fe:0,03 Zn:0,1 Col.:0 Hsr.:0

Quantity of ingredients:
Green tea 1 teaspoon / 2g. (yes)
Water 1 cup / 120g. (yes)

Cooking instructions:
For each cup you use a teaspoonful or a teabag.
Pour green tea only with 60 to 80 ° C / 140 to 176 °F hot water, otherwise it will be bitter.
If the tea has a stimulating effect, let it draw for two to three minutes. It has a calming effect for a duration of five minutes (no longer, otherwise it will be bitter!).
Another method: Pour the tea leaves with about 70 ° C / 158 °F hot water and pour the water immediately again. Then just pour hot water again. The bitter substances disappear and the tea gets a milder aroma.

9.44 Tea mixture against general exhaustion

Good to fight general exhaustion. Antibacterial, encouragingly, good to fight loss of appetite, flatulence, heartburn.
Cooking time approx. 10 min
4 portions to 127g. / 2kcal. - (carb:55% / prot:45%)
100g.=1,57kcal. / protein 0,17g. fat:0,04g.
µg. - Ph:0,46 Na:0,43 Ka:3,71 Mg:0,53 Ca:2,53 Fe:0 Zn:0,03 Col.:0 Hsr.:0

Quantity of ingredients:
Lemon Balm (dried) 2 teaspoons / 3g. (yes)
Blackberry leaves 2 teaspoons / 3g. (yes)
Lavender blossoms 1 teaspoon / 2g. (yes)
Water 1 1/2 cups / 500g. (yes)

Cooking instructions:
Heat the water till it boils and put it aside. Add 2 g lemon balm, 2 g blackberry leaves, 1,5g lavender flowers, leave to stand covered for 10 minutes, then strain. Drink a cup three times a day.

9.45 Tea rooibos

Antioxidant, anti-inflammatory, anticancer, flavonoids, it also has a positive effect on Alzheimer, arteriosclerosis. Antiallergic, inhibits histamine release. Antibacterial, antiviral, antifungal, detoxifying (alkaline).
Cooking time approx. 10 min.
5 portions to 200,8g. / 0kcal. - (carb:0% / prot:0%)
100g.=0kcal. / protein 0g. fat:0g.
µg. - Ph:0 Na:0,04 Ka:0 Mg:0,04 Ca:0,2 Fe:0 Zn:0 Col.:0 Hsr.:0

Quantity of ingredients:
Rooibos tea 4 teaspoons / 4g. (rec.)
Water 4 cup / 1000g. (yes)

Cooking instructions:
Brew 3-4 teaspoons of rooibos with one liter of boiling water and leave for 6-10 minutes. With soft water you use less tea for the preparation, with harder water we recommend a higher dosage.

9.46 Tomato with mozzarella

Promotes digestion, helps to digest fat, supports urination, reduces blood pressure. Affects anorexia, good to fight flatulence, inflammatory bowel disease, bloating and nausea. Relaxing and reassuring.
Cooking time approx. 5 min
Allergens: AG
1 portion to 217g. / 436kcal. - (carb:37% / prot:63%)
100g.=200,92kcal. / protein 14,85g. fat:30,31g.
µg. - Ph:90,53 Na:176,32 Ka:158,47 Mg:12,75 Ca:109,48 Fe:0,33 Zn:0,5 Col.:10,69 Hsr.:13,46

Quantity of ingredients:
Mozzarella 1 piece / 50g. (little)
Tomato 2 pieces / 100g. (little)
Salt 1 pinch / 1g. (little)
Basil (fresh) 5 leaves / 6g. (yes)
Olive oil 2 table spoons / 20g. (little)
White bread (wheat bread) 2 slices / 40g. (yes)

Cooking instructions:
Cut tomatoes and mozzarella into slices. Serve with salt, basil and olive oil. Serve with white bread.

10 Effects of food

10.1 Use ingredients: recommendable

Acai powder
Anise (Common Fennel)
Asparagus (green or white)
Aubergine
Banana
Banana (cooking banana)
Basic recipe for a beef soup
Basic recipe for a beef soup (warming)
Basic recipe for a chicken soup (warming)
Basic recipe for a fish soup
Basic recipe for a rice soup (Congee)
Basic recipe for a vegetable soup (nutritious)
Bitter Herb liqueur
Black caraway
Blackberry´s
Blue mallow tee
Cantaloupe
Carrot
Carrot (Early Carrot)
Carrot juice without sugar
Celery root
Chamomile tea
Chervil
Chervil dried
Chinese pearl barley
Codfish
Cottage cheese
Cream 10% coffee cream
Cress
Crucian
Dill
Elderberries
Elderberry blossom tee
Fennel
Fennel seeds ground
Fennel tea
Fox nut, gorgon nut, makhana
Gourd
Ground
Ground caraway
Herbal tea mix
Hibiscus
Hokkaido pumpkin
Kudzu
Lamb's lettuce
Lily bulbs
Loquate / Japanese medlar
Lotus roots
Lotus seeds
Lovage
Mascarpone cheese
Parsley
Parsley root
Potato
Potato (mealy)
Pumpkin
Red beet
Spinach
Turmeric (yellow root)
Turnips
Watermelon
Wax gourd
Zucchini

10.2 Use ingredients: yes

Aloe juice
Amaranth
Amaranth Pops
Angelica root
Apple puree
Arrowroot
Artichoke
Baking powder
Balm
Bamboo shoots
Banchatee (green tea)
barberry
Barley
Barley flour
Barley grass powder
Barley grouts
Barley malt
Barley not peeled
Basil
Basil (fresh)
Batavia
Bay leaf
Berries of the season
Blackberry leaves
Blueberry
Borage

Boxhorn clover seeds
Bread roll
Bread with carob kernel flour
Breadcrumbs (wheat bread, bread roll)
Broccoli
Buckbean
Buckwheat
Buckwheat (roasted) Kasha
Bulgur (cereals)
Burdock root tea
Butter (half fat)
Butter Bio
Buttermilk
Calamari
Carambola (Star fruit)
Cardamom
Carob flour, St. john's bread
Celery sticks
Cereal coffee
Chamomile
Channa-Dal
Chard
Chicken egg white
Chickweed
Chicory
Chlorella (fresh water)
Chrysanthemum blossom tea
Cinnamon ground
Cinnamon sticks
Clove
Cod
Coix (seeds) YiYi Ren
Compote (fruits of the season)
Coriander
Coriander (fresh)
Corn
Corn (fast polenta)
Corn (roasted)
Corn flour
Corn Grease (Polenta)
Corn silk tea
Corn starch
Couscous
Cow's milk (1.5% fat)
Crab
Cranberry
Cranberry
Cranberry jam
Cranberry juice
Cream sour 10%
Creamer
Crispbread
Cumin (Caraway seed)
Curcuma

Curd cheese 20%
Currant (black)
Currant (red)
Currant (white)
Daisy
Dandelion (young plants)
Dandelion juice
Dandelionroots tea
Dashi
Dulse (seaweed)
Endive salad
Fenugreek (Trigonella foenum-graecum)
Feta cheese
Fig
Fish pieces mixed (fresh water)
Flounder
Flower pollen
Freshwater crab
Freshwater fish
Fruit tea
Galangal
Gelatin white
Gelee Royal
Gentian root
Gentian root tea
Ginkgo fruit
Ginseng
Ginseng root
Goat and sheep's milk
Goat cheese
Gooseberry
Green tea
Guava
Halibut (Flatfish)
Hawthorn
Herbs bitter
Herbs of Provence
Herbs various
Herbs wild
Hibiscus tea
Hijiki
Hyssop
Iceberg lettuce
Jasmine blossoms tee
Jellyfish
Juniper berry
Kalmus
Kefir
King Solomon's-seal
Kohlrabi
Kukicha tea
Kumquats
Ladyfingers

Lamb's lettuce
Lavender blossoms
Leaf salads (bitter)
Lemon Balm (dried)
Lemon Balm (fresh)
Lemongrass
Lettuce
Licorice root tea
Lime blossom tea
Liver smoothing tea
Lobster
Longane
Lovage seeds
Luo Han Guo fruit
Lychee
Lychee in Preserved
Lye roll
Mallow (Malva sylvestris) blossom tea
Mare's milk
Marjoram
Mediterranean fish (cod, plaice, haddock, sea eel, mackerel)
Medlar
Millet
Millet flakes
Mineral water
Miso
Miso black (fermented)
Mulberry fruit
Mulled Wine Spice
Mullet
Mussels
Nasturtium (nose-twister or nose-tweaker)
Nettles
Noodles (wheat) with egg
Noodles (wheat, lasagne) with egg
Noodles (wheat, ribbon noodles) with egg
Noodles (wheat, spaghetti) with egg
Nori, purple seaweed, red algae
Nutmeg
Oat
Oat flour
Oat fusion (baby food)
Oat milk
Octopus
Octopus
Okra
Orange blossom
Oregano dried
Oregano fresh
Oysters
Papaya

Parsnip
Passion blossoms tea
Passion fruit
Pearl barley
Pearl barley
Peppermint
Peppermint tea
Perch
Pimento
Plaice
Pomegranate
Potato flour
Prickly pear
Processed cheese 12%
Pudding powder vanilla
Quince
Quinoa
Radicchio
Radish black
Radish leaves
Raspberry
Raspberry leaf tea
Red berry (without sugar)
Rhubarb
Ribworttea
Rice (fragrance)
Rice (Gaoliang / Sorghum)
Rice Basmati
Rice flour
Rice long grain rice
Rice malt
Rice mash
Rice noodles
Rice red
Rice round grain
Rice starch
Rice sticky
Rice sweet
Rice variety any
Romaine lettuce / lettuce salad
Rose blossom tea
Rose hip
Rose hip tea
Rose leaf tea
Rosefish
Rosemary
Rucola
Rusk
Rye
Rye flour
Safflower (Dyer's thistle / Hong Hua)
Saffron
Sage
Sago (cereals)

Salmon
Salsify
Sea buckthorn
Seacrab
Shark
Sheep's milk
Sheep's milk yoghurt
Shrimp
Shrimps
Skim milk powder
Slug
Sorrel
Sour cream 15% fat
Sour milk
Sour milk cheese 20%
Sourdough
Spelled flakes
Spelled grain
Spelled semolina
Spiny lobsters
Spurdog (spiny dogfish, Schillerlocken)
Star anise
Stevia (candyleaf, sweetleaf)
Strawberries
Sugar substitute (sweetener)
Supplementary nutrition
Sweet potato
Tarragon (Estragon)
Tea mixture uric acid lowering
Thyme
Thyme dried
Topinambur
Trout
Tsampa (roasted barley flour)

Turnip
Valerian
Vanilla
Vanilla pod
Vanilla powder
Wakame
Water
Water hot
Wheat
Wheat bulgur
Wheat flakes
Wheat flatbread/pita bread
Wheat flour
Wheat semolina
Wheat semolina for children
Wheatgrass juice
Wheatgrass powder
Whey
White bread (baguette)
White bread (pretzel sticks)
White bread (roll)
White bread (wheat bread)
White breadcrumbs
White dumpling bread (wheat bread cut into chunks)
Whitefish
Wild herbs
Wild strawberries
Wormwood herb
Yam root, yam root tuber
Yarrow
Yarrow tea
Yogi tea
Yogurt (natural, 1.5% fat)

10.3 Use ingredients: little

Acerola fruit nectar or powder
Agar agar (kelp)
Agave nectar
Apple (sour)
Apple (sweet)
Apple juice (natural cloudy)
Apricot jam
Avocado
Bean oil
Bearberry leaf
Beef fillet
Beef meat
Beef meat (calf)
Beef meatbones
Beef Oxtail pieces
Beef soup meat

Berry juice
Blackberry jam
Blueberry dried
Blueberry jam
Blueberry juice
Borage oil
Buckwheat whole grain
Capers in olive oil
Cauliflower
Caviar
Chestnut puree
Chestnuts
Chicken egg
Chicken meat
Chicken yolk
Clarified butter

Cocoa
Cooking oil
Corn germ oil
Cow's milk (whole milk 3.5% fat)
Cranberries
Cream sour 20%
Cucumber
Cucumber (bitter)
Cucumber (spicy cucumber)
Curd cheese 40%
Currant jam (black)
Currant jam (red)
Currant juice (black)
Currants (black)
Currants (red)
Dates dried
Dates red
Deer meat
Deer meat
Deer's Bones
Ducks egg
Edam cheese
Feta cheese
Fig dried
Fish innards
Fish remains
Fish sauce
Fresh cheese
Fresh cheese from soya
Fresh cheese with herbs
Fructose (glucose)
Fruit mix juice
Goat
Goose egg
Gouda cheese
Grape juice red
Grape juice white
Grapes red
Grapes white
Grapeseed oil
Grass carp
Green spelt
Herring
Honey
Hop
Horse meat
Kiwi
Kombu seaweed (Saccharina japonica)
Lamb bones
Lamb meat
Lamb shoulder
Linseed oil
Mackerel
Malt

Mango
Mango juice
Maple syrup
Margarine
Margarine (diet)
Mold cheese
Mozzarella
Multi-grain bread (gray bread)
Mustard seeds
Mutton
Mutton
Nectarine
Oat flakes roasted
Oat meal
Olive oil
Orange jam
Palm oil
Peaches
Peaches (canned)
Peanut oil
Pear
Pear juice
Pheasant
Pigeon
Pigeon egg
Pineapple
Pineapple (from a can)
Pineapple juice without sugar
Poppy
Pork ham
Pork ham cooked
Pork ham smoked
Pork knuckle
Pork meat
processed cheese 30%
Pumpkin seed oil
Quail
Quail egg
Rabbit
Rabbit (wild)
Rabbit meat
Raisins
Rapeseed oil
Raspberry dried (immature)
Raspberry jam
Salt
Salt (herbal)
Sesame oil
Soy flour
Soy noodles
Soy sauce
Soy Tofu
Soy Tofu smoked
Soybean milk

Soybean oil
Spelled (Dark) bread
Spelled wholemeal flour
St. Benedict's thistle, blessed thistle, holy thistle, spotted thistle
Strawberry jam
Strawberry Juice
Sugar - icing sugar
Sugar brown
Sugar candy white
Sugar cane sugar
Sugar fructose - fruit sugar
Sugar glucose - grapes sugar
Sugar Milk Sugar
Sugar molasses
Sugar palm sugar
Sugar white
Sunflower oil
Thistle oil
Tomato
Tomato juice
Tomato paste
Tomato puree
Tonic Water
Truffle
Tuna
Turkey breast meat
Turkey ham
Umeboshi paste
Vanilla sugar natural
Vegetable juice
Vinegar (Apple vinegar)
Vinegar (Red wine vinegar)
Vinegar Aceto Balsamico
Vinegar Aceto Balsamico white
Walnut oil
Wheat germ oil
Wild boar meat
Yeast
Yoghurt vanilla
Yogurt (natural, 3.5% fat)

10.4 Do not use contra-acting foods

Adzuki beans
Agrimony
Almond
Almond marzipan
Almond milk
Almond puree
Anchovy / Sardine
Apricot
Apricot dried
Apricot nectar
Apricots
Apricots juice
Basic recipe for a duck soup
Beans (green, fresh)
Beef bone marrow
Beef heart
Beef heart (calf)
Beef kidney
Beef liver
Beef lungs (calf)
Beef stomach
Beer (alcohol-free)
Beer (alcohol-reduced)
Beer (Pils)
Beer (Top-fermented German dark beer)
Bitter Lemon
Bitter liqueur

Contraindicated food

Bitter orange peel
Black beans
Black fungus mushroom
Black tea
Blackberry dried (unripe fruit)
Black-eyed peas
Blackthorn (Sloe)
Bocksdorn fruits (Fructus Lycii, Goji, goji berry
Boletus mushroom
Brazil nuts
Brie cheese
Broad beans (thick beans)
Brown ale
Brussels sprouts
Bush beans
Butter beans white
Camembert
Campari
Carp
Cashews
Champignon
Chanterelle
Chenpi (chinese tangerine bowl)
Cherry
Cherry (sour)
Cherry compote
Cherry juice
Chicken Blood
Chicken heart

Chicken liver
Chicken stomach
Chickpeas
Chili (pod or ground)
Chinese cabbage
Chives
Chocolate
Chocolate (Diabetic)
Clementine
Clementines
Coconut fat
Coconut flakes
Coconut grated
Coconut meat
Coconut milk
Coffee
Cola drink
Cola drink (low calorie)
Cream (30% fat)
Cream sour 30%
Cream, sweet 30%
Creme fraiche cheese
Curry
Curry paste red
Deer's kidneys
Duck (heart)
Duck (slaughtered)
Dyer's broom herb
Eel
Eel smoked
Emmental cheese
Evening primrose oil
Fernet Branca (herbal bitter liqueur)
French beans
Gail plum
Garam Masala powder
Garlic
Ginger fresh
Ginger oil
Ginger powder
Ginseng liqueur
Goat and sheep's blood
Goat and sheep's brain
Goat and sheep's liver
Goat and sheep's stomach
Goose
Goose blood
Goose fat
Goose parts
Gorgonzola
Grapefruit (Pomelo)
Grapefruit dried peel
Grapefruit juice
Greengage

Hazelnuts
Honey wine (Met)
Horehound leaves
Kaki plum
Kidney beans (red)
Lamb kidneys
Lamb liver
Leek
Lemon
Lemon juice
Lemon peel
Lentils
Lentils black
Lentils red
Lentils yellow
Lima beans
Lime
Linseed
Linseed (crushed)
Lychee liqueur
Manioc flour
Martini
Mayonnaise 50%
Mayonnaise 80%
Mirabelle plum
Miso paste (soy bean paste)
Mixed Pickles
Morel (black, dried)
Morel, dried
Mu Erh Mushroom
Muesli
Mung bean
Mung bean sprouting
Mustard
Mustard Dijon
Mustard medium hot
Mustard sweet
Noodles (whole grain) with egg
Oat flakes (whole grain)
Olives
Olives green
Onion (shallot)
Onion (spring onion)
Onion read
Onion white
Orange
Orange dried peel
Orange grated peel
Orange juice
Orange peel
Oyster mushroom
Oyster shell powder
Parmesan
Peanut (roasted)

Peanut butter
Peanuts
Peas
Peas, green
Pepper (ground)
Pepper Cayenne
Pepper powder (hot)
Pepper white (ground)
Peppercorns
Pepperoni
Pepperoni, red, pitted, halved
Pepperoni, yellow, pitted, halved
Peppers
Peppers (rose peppers)
Peppers (sweet)
Peppers powder
Pickle
Pig blood
Pine nuts
Pinto beans speckled
Pistachios
Plum
Plum dried
Plums
Pork Bacon
Pork brain
Pork fat (lard)
Pork heart
Pork kidneys
Pork Lard
Pork liver
Pork lung
Pork marrow bones
Pork sausage (Bratwurst)
Pork skin
Pork stomach
Pork/beef sausage (smoked)
Pork's intestine
Prosecco
Psyllium seed
Puff pastry
Pumpernickel (dark bread)
Pumpkin seeds
Rabbit liver
Radish
Radish (white, green, purple-red)
Radish horseradish

Red cabbage
Red wine
Reishi mushroom
Rice (whole grain)
Rice black
Rice wild (nature rice)
Rum
Rye wholemeal bread
Sake
Sauerkraut (cutted cabbage fermented)
Savory
Savoy cabbage / kale
Sea cucumber
Sesame oil roasted
Sesame paste (Tahini)
Sesame, black
Sesame, white
Sherry (whine)
Shiitake, dried
Sour cherries
Soya Cuisine (soy cream)
Soybeans
Soybeans, black
Soybeans, blacks, fermented
Soybeans, yellow
Spirit
Sunflower seeds
Tabasco
Tangerine
Toast bread (whole grain)
Tomato dried
Trout (smoked)
Umeboshi plums (Japanese apricots)
Walnuts
Walnuts roasted
Wheat beer
Wheat bran
Wheat flour whole grain
Wheat/Rye/Gray-black bread with yeast
White beans
White cabbage
White wine
Whole grain bread
Wholemeal flour
Wild garlic (garlic spinach)
Wormwood
Yew nut

11 Complementary

11.1 xx

xx

12 Basics of Nutrition

The basic principles of nutrition described herein are general recommendations. They are not aimed at a specific form of therapy. Recommendations concerning a therapy have priority.

12.1 Nutrition

Regular meals in a relaxed atmosphere. A warm breakfast is considered a good start into the day.
The main meals ought to be taken for lunch – supper in the early evening. Pay attention to feeling hungry or sated: don't eat too much nor remain hungry is the rule
Prepare the meals freshly from natural, regional products. Frozen, heat-conserved, industrially prepared or foodstuffs cooked in the microwave oven are rejected.
Choice of foodstuffs according to the season: more cooling food in summer, more warming food in winter.
Eat cooked food at least twice a day. Food and drinks ought to be lukewarm, never ice-cold or hot.
Raw vegetables, briefly cooked vegetables, freshly squeezed juices and mineral water are not recommended. Milk and dairy products are only included in the diet if they don't cause problems.
Don't use therapeutic recipes over a longer period without consulting your doctor or therapist.

Varied food
Enjoy the diversity of foodstuffs. Characteristics of a balanced nutrition are variety, suitable combination and a balanced quantity of rich and low energy foodstuffs (on one hand avoiding undersupply with essential nutrients and on the other hand to take to many undesirable substances).

A lot of Cereal Products - and Potatoes
Bread, pasta, rice, cereal flakes (best wholemeal) as well as potatoes contain almost no fat, but many vitamins, mineral nutrients, trace elements, roughage and secondary plant substances. These foodstuffs ought to be taken with low-fat side dishes.

Vegetables and Fruit – „Take Five" every day …
5 portions of vegetables and fruit a day, as fresh as possible, briefly cooked, or maybe one portion as a juice – ideal as a side dish to every meal as well as snack between meals: Thus a lot of vitamins, mineral nutrients as well as roughage and secondary plant substances

Daily milk and dairy products
Milk and Dairy Products every Day, once or twice per Week Fish; meat, sausages as well as eggs moderately. These foodstuffs contain valuable nutrients like calcium in the milk, iodine selenium and omega-3 fat acids in saltwater fish. Meat is favorable due to its high content of disposable iron and the vitamins B1, B6 and B12. Quantities of 300 – 600 g meat and sausage per week are sufficient. Prefer low-fat products, especially in meat- and dairy products.

Low-fat and fatty Foodstuffs
Fat supplies us with essential fat acids and fatty foodstuffs contain also fat-soluble vitamins. Fat is high in energy; therefore much fat in the food may cause overweight, possibly also cancer. Too many saturated fat acids may further a tendency for cardio-vascular diseases in the long term. Prefer vegetable oils and fats (e.g. rapeseed-, olive-, soya-oils and solid fats produced therefrom). Beware of invisible fat in meat- and dairy products, pastry and sweets as well as in fast-food and convenience foods. 70 – 90 g fat per day is sufficient.

Moderately Sugar and Salt
Take sugar and foods/drinks containing various kinds of sugar (e.g. glucose syrup) only occasionally. Use herbs and spices as well as a little salt creatively. Prefer salt containing iodine.

Plenty of Liquids
Water is absolutely essential. Drink 1-2 l liquids every day. Prefer water (with or without gas) and other low-calorie drinks. Alcoholic drinks should not be taken.

Tasty Dishes, carefully cooked
Cook the meals with as low temperatures and as short as possible, using little water and fat – this preserves the original taste, keeps the nutrients intact and prevents the production of harmful compounds.

Take time and enjoy the food
Take your Time and enjoy your Food
Eating consciously helps to eat right. The eye enjoys food, too. It's fun, invites to enjoy varied dishes and stimulates the feeling of satiety.

Watch your Weight and stay in Motion
A balanced diet and a lot of exercise and sport (30 – 60 min/day) are a healthy combination. The right weight furthers well-being and health. Thermals, directional effectiveness, digestive power

There are various criteria for judging the effectiveness of herbs and foodstuffs.
The use of certain herbs and ingredients is based on observations of the effects on the body which these foodstuffs, herbs and spices show after having eaten them. The medical science has developed following system: Every ingredient or herb has a directional effectiveness. Furthermore, there are herbs which have a special effect on certain organs.
The basic condition for a healthy metabolism is to obtain sufficient energy from food and that the digestive process doesn't use too much energy. An easily digestible meal makes content and sated, doesn't cause flatulence and fatigue after the meal. The perfect spices increase the healthiness of our meals. Very often, just small doses of herbs and spices will suffice. They are not used to make us sated, but to help our digestive organs to digest the food.

12.2 Recipes

The recipes list the ingredients to be used and the cooking instructions show how the dish is prepared. The list of ingredients shows the concerned quantities as well as the relevance for the therapy. If you find „less than mentioned", try to comply or find an alternative from the „list of recommended foodstuffs". Mostly it shall result just in a small change of taste when you simply avoid this ingredient.
Mild cooking methods: boiling, stewing, poaching, steaming
Strong cooking methods: barbecuing, roasting, frying, smoking
Balanced cooking methods: deep-frying, baking brick
Deep-freezing and warming in the microwave oven should be avoided (denaturalization).

12.3 Foodstuffs

Foodstuffs have an effect on body and soul like medicinal herbs, only a very much milder one. Dietary advice is mainly based on regional foodstuffs. The knowledge about the effects of each foodstuff and the knowledge, when which foodstuff shall be used, is based on the orthodox school of medicine. Use ecologic-organic products, if possible. As everything should be cooked for a long time due to a better digestability and very rarely eaten raw, the food agrees with everyone.
The classification of the foodstuffs according to their effect on the body is the basis in order to achieve a harmonious status of health.

Dietary advisors do not recommend certain foodstuffs for everyone. The individual diet is tailor-made for the individual constitution.

Buy only fresh and ripe fruit and vegetables. You ought to leave unripe fruit and vegetables and such with brown spots and wilted leaves behind in the market. In this case take deep-frozen goods (never ready-to-serve dishes!). Fruit and vegetables are deep-frozen immediately after harvesting and often contain more vitamins and minerals than the goods from the vegetable shelf. Whereas conserved or tinned goods contain very much less biological substances. Also, salt, sugar and others are mostly added to the latter. Never leave the foodstuffs in the water after washing them to avoid that many vital substances get drowned. Clean salads, fruit and vegetables immediately before serving.

Please make sure of the hygienic processing of foodstuffs. Clean your salads, fruit and vegetables carefully. When cooking with meat, prepare all ingredients first and then process the meat products. Clean the worktop and tools very carefully. Wooden surfaces ought to be treated with a mild disinfectant regularly in order to reduce germination.

Store fruit and vegetables separately, if possible. Harvested fruit and vegetables are still alive and emit e.g. ethylene gas, which makes other products ripen and age faster. Keep meat and fish in the closed packaging or store them in the fridge in closed containers.

12.4 Herbs

There are some basic rules for storing medicinal herbs. On principle, herbs must be protected from direct sunlight, humidity and heat.

Containers for the storage of herbs may be glasses, ceramic jars and even plastic containers. However, plastic is a rather unsuitable material and should only be a short-term solution. In case of glass containers, use a dark material.

Medicinal herbs cannot be kept for any long period. The shelf life of herbs is limited. However, it can be prolonged with suitable storage. The place should be dark, rather cool and absolutely dry. A wooden medicine cabinet, placed not directly next to a source of heat, would be ideal. Never buy large quantities of herbs so as not to have to throw them away. Label the container with the name of the herb and the date of harvesting or processing.

13 Other dietic-books

The following syndromes of dietetics, TCM or for a therapy supplement for cancer are available.

Dietetics

E001. Nutrition of the infant - baby food
E002. Nutrition during lactation
E003. Nutrition in old age
E004. Nutrition of children and adolescents
E005. Nutrition of athletes
E006. Light weight
E007. Pregnancy
E008. Full food

Protein and electrolyte - kidneys
E009. (hemodialysis) dialysis treatment
E010. Acute renal failure
E011. Chronic renal insufficiency
E012. Nephrotic syndrome
E013. Kidney stones (nephrolithiasis)

Gastrointestinal tract - pancreas
E014. Acute pancreatitis (inflammation of the pancreas)
E015. Chronic pancreatitis (inflammation of the pancreas)

Gastrointestinal tract - small intestine and large intestine
E016. Acute obstipation (constipation)
E017. Chronic obstipation (constipation)
E018. Colon irritabile
E019. Diverticulitis
E020. Acquired lactose intolerance (lactose malabsorption)
E021. Fructose malabsorption
E022. Glutensensitive enteropathy (celiac disease)
E023. Colectomy
E024. Short Bowel Syndrome

Gastrointestinal tract - liver, gallbladder, bile ducts
E025. Acute and chronic hepatitis (inflammation of the liver)
E026. Cholelithiasis (bile stones)
E027. fatty liver
E028. cirrhosis

Gastrointestinal tract - Stomach and duodenal intestine
E029. Acute gastritis
E030. Chronic gastritis
E031. Stomach bleeding
E032. Ulcus ventriculi and duodenal ulcer
E033. Condition after gastric surgery

Gastrointestinal tract - oral cavity and esophagus
E034. Stomatitis
E035. Esophageal carcinoma (esophageal cancer)
E036. Refluosophagitis (heartburn)

Special diseases
E037. Phenylketonuria (PKU)
E038. Rheumatic joint diseases

Metabolism
E039. Obesity (overweight)
E040. Diabetes mellitus
E041. Eating disorders (underweight)

Fat metabolism
E042. Hypercholesterolaemia (increased cholesterol level)
E043. Hepatic Encephalopathy

Heart and circulation
E044. Arteriosclerosis (arterial calcification)
E045. Heart insufficiency
E046. Hypertension
E047. Hyperuricaemia and gout

Changed nutrient requirements
E048. In case of fever
E049. For malignant diseases
E050. After burns
E051. Radiation and chemotherapy

CANCER
E100. Pancreatic cancer
E101. Bladder cancer
E102. Blood cancer (leukemia)
E103. Breast cancer
E104. Colorectal cancer
E105. Gastric cancer
E106. Kidney cancer
E107. Esophageal cancer

TCM
E200. Bladder - moisture heat in the bladder
E201. Bladder - moisture and cold in the bladder
E202. Bladder - emptiness and cold in the bladder
E203. Large intestine - external cold affects the large intestine
E204. Large intestine - moisture heat in the large intestine
E205. Large intestine - heat blocks the intestine II acute
E206. Large intestine - dryness of the colon
E207. Large intestine - Yang deficiency (cold)
E208. Heart - Blood insufficiency
E209. Heart - Blood stagnation
E210. Heart - Fire
E211. Heart - Hot mucus clogs the heart pores

E212. Heart - Cold mucus clogs the heart pores
E213. Heart - Qi deficiency
E214. Heart - Yang deficiency
E215. Heart - Yin deficiency
E216. Liver - Ascending Liver Yang
E217. Liver - Blood deficiency
E218. Liver - Blood stagnation
E219. Liver - Moisture heat in liver and gall bladder
E220. Liver - Fire
E221. Liver - Gall bladder Qi-Empty
E222. Liver - Cold in the liver meridian
E223. Liver - Qi stagnation
E224. Liver - Wind
E225. Liver - Wind with ascending liver Yang
E226. Liver - Wind with blood anemic
E227. Liver - Wind with extreme heat
E228. Lung - Qi deficiency
E229. Lung - Mucus-moisture in the lungs
E230. Lung - Mucus-heat in the lungs
E231. Lung - Mucus-cold in the lungs
E232. Lung - Dryness of the lungs
E233. Lung - Wind-heat attacks the lungs
E234. Lung - Wind-cold affects the lungs
E235. Lung - Yin deficiency
E236. Stomach - Bloodstagnation
E237. Stomach - Fire
E238. Stomach - Cold with liquid
E239. Stomach - Nutrition stagnation
E240. Stomach - Qi deficiency
E241. Stomach - Rebellious Qi
E242. Stomach - Yin Emptiness
E243. Spleen - Heat and moisture attack the spleen
E244. Spleen - Coldness and moisture affects the spleen
E245. Spleen - Qi deficiency
E246. Spleen - Qi deficiency + Declining spleen Qi
E247. Spleen - Qi deficiency + spleen does not control the blood
E248. Spleen - Yang deficiency
E249. Kidney - Heart and kidney no longer communicate
E250. Kidney - Jing deficiency
E251. Kidney - Kidneys cannot receive the Qi
E252. Kidney - Qi is not stable
E253. Kidney - Yang deficiency
E254. Kidney - Yin deficiency

For further information visit di-book.com.

14 EBNS - Software for nutritional counseling

The main task of the database is to create personalized nutritional advice for each patient individually. The database was developed for Dietetics and Traditional Chinese Medicine.

The Database supports training and advices in the daily work routine.

The computer program provides lists of recipes, ingredients and herbs, which are given to the client. individually adjustable according to patient's request from whole food to vegetarians (lacto, ovo, ...). For every register there is an information sheet which can be given to the client. All texts can be individually designed.

The syndromes can be combined and result in an intersection of the recommended recipes and ingredients. The automated diagnosis for the TCM enables you to check your experience during the training as well as to confirm your diagnosis in the working day. You select several predefined symptoms and have the program automatically display the relevant syndromes.

How to work with the database:
Select the patient / client, select one or more of the syndromes you diagnosed and print the folder.

You can change all values, create new symptoms or syndromes, develop recipes, change or adapt ingredients and herbs to your findings. In simple client management, all relevant data about the person is stored. You get an overview of the past diagnoses and the development of the course of the disease.

As a consultant you save a lot of time when you print out the recipe, food and herbal lists for the recognized syndromes and give them to the clients. You can use this time for a personal conversation. With the database, dieticians and nutritionists can view the nutrients and trace elements for each recipe and develop recipes for syndromes even with suggested ingredients.

All recipe and grocery lists can also be ordered from me as a combination of several diseases. I wish all readers good luck, health and happiness in life.
More information can be found at www.ebns.at.
Volunteer: www.krebsinfo.at
Josef Miligui